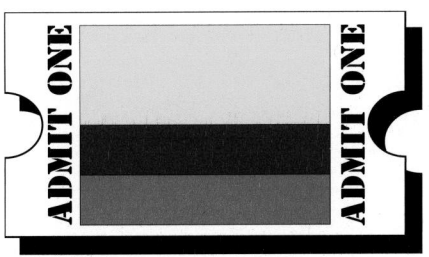

Coffee Plants
Growing Near
Armenia

FACES
AND
PLACES

COLOMBIA

BY CALEB OWENS

THE CHILD'S WORLD®

COVER PHOTO

A smiling girl on Providence Island.
©Macduff Everton/CORBIS

Published in the United States of America by The Child's World®
PO Box 326
Chanhassen, MN 55317-0326
800-599-READ
www.childsworld.com

Project Manager James R. Rothaus/James R. Rothaus & Associates
Designer Robert E. Bonaker/R. E. Bonaker & Associates
Contributors Mary Berendes, Dawn M. Dionne, Katherine Stevenson, Ph.D., Red Line Editorial

The Child's World® and Faces and Places are the sole property
and registered trademarks of The Child's World®.

Library of Congress Cataloging-in-Publication Data
Owens, Caleb.
Colombia / by Caleb Owens.
p. cm.
Includes index.
ISBN 1-56766-905-0 (lib. bdg. : alk. paper)
1. Colombia—Juvenile Literature.
[1. Colombia]
I. Title.
F2258.5 .O94 2003
986.1—dc21

*J980.1
Owes*

00-013156

Table of Contents

CHAPTER	PAGE
Where Is Colombia?	6
The Land	9
Plants and Animals	10
Long Ago	13
Colombia Today	14
The People	17
City Life and Country Life	18
Schools and Language	21
Work	22
Food	25
Pastimes and Holidays	26
Country Facts	28
Colombia Trivia	30
Glossary	31
Index and Web Sites	32

Planet Earth has seven large areas of land surrounded by vast blue oceans. These land areas are called **continents**. Colombia is a nation at the northwest corner of the continent of South America.

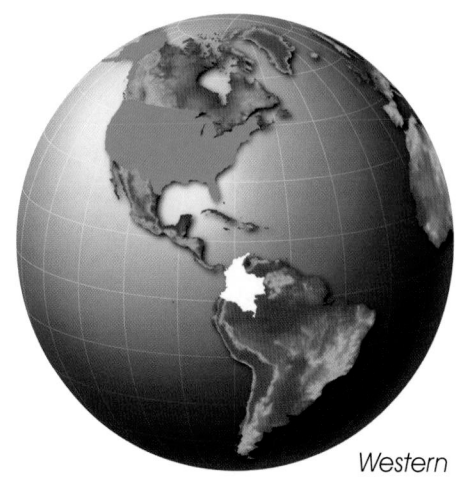

Western Hemisphere

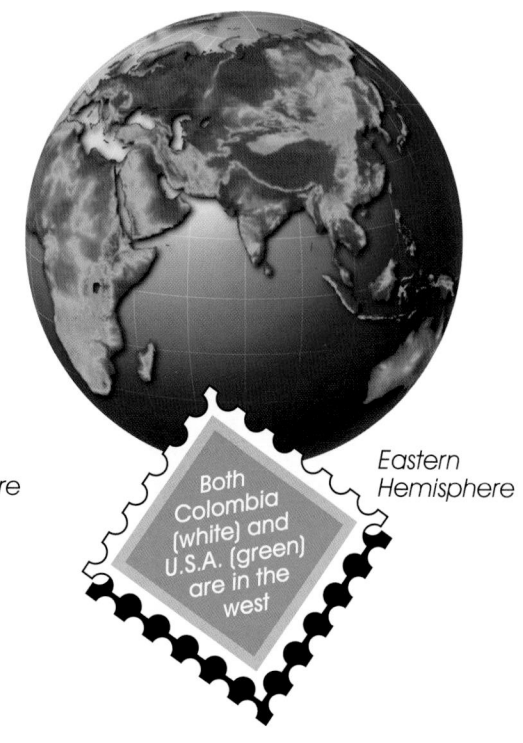

Eastern Hemisphere

Both Colombia (white) and U.S.A. (green) are in the west

The northern and western sides of Columbia are bordered by the Caribbean Sea and the Pacific Ocean. Separating the two is long, thin Panama, the southernmost nation in Central America. Columbia's other neighbors are Venezuela to the east, Ecuador and Peru to the south, and huge Brazil to the southeast.

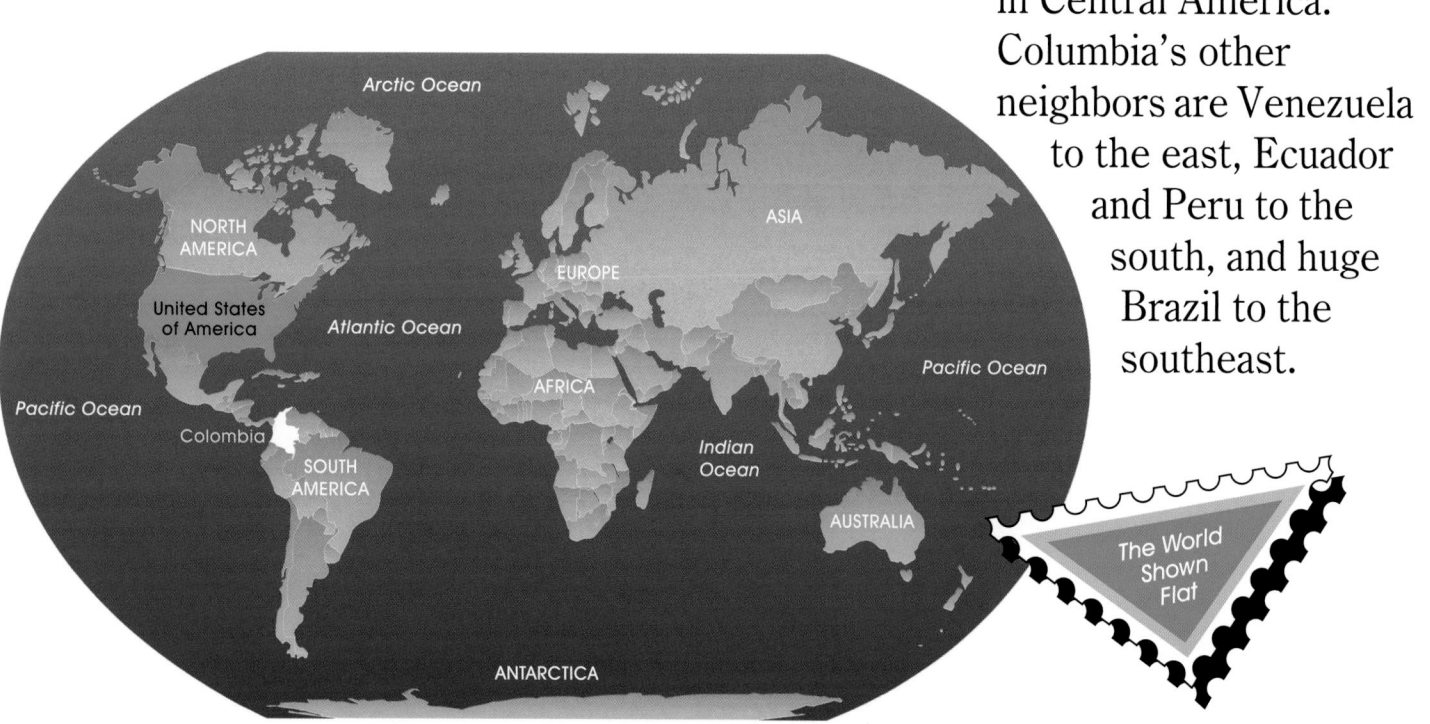

Arctic Ocean

NORTH AMERICA

United States of America

Atlantic Ocean

ASIA

EUROPE

AFRICA

Pacific Ocean

Pacific Ocean

Colombia

SOUTH AMERICA

Indian Ocean

AUSTRALIA

ANTARCTICA

The World Shown Flat

Close-Up
of
Colombia

Caribbean Sea

PANAMA

VENEZUELA

*Pacific
Ocean*

COLOMBIA

ECUADOR

BRAZIL

PERU

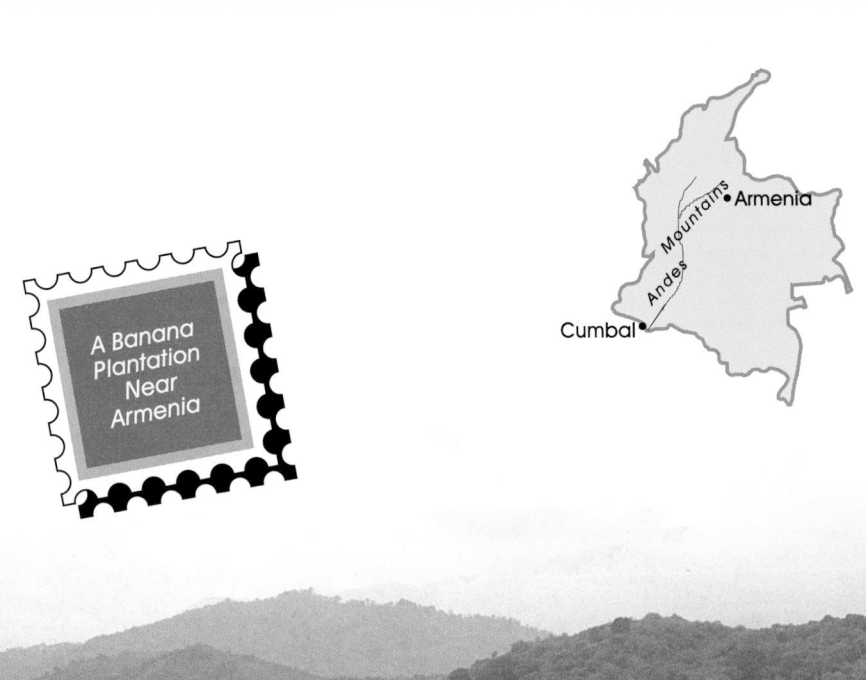

A Banana
Plantation
Near
Armenia

Armenia

Mountains

Andes

Cumbal

©Enzo & Paolo Ragazzini/CORBIS

Colombia is a land of incredible differences. The seacoast has sandy beaches and scenic islands. Just inland are the snow-capped ranges of the Andes Mountains. The mountains are divided by two deep valleys where most of Colombia's people live.

Northeastern Colombia has deserts, while the east has huge, flat grasslands called *llanos* (YAHN-ose). South of the *llanos* are the thick jungles of the Amazon rain forest.

Colombia's weather varies as much as its landscape. Colombia is on the **equator**, the imaginary line that runs around Earth's center. Countries near the equator tend to have hot, moist, **tropical** weather all year long. Some parts of Colombia are certainly hot and moist. But the higher, mountainous areas are much cooler. Other parts of the country are dry.

Cumbal Volcano

©Kevin Schafer/CORBIS

Plants & Animals

ADMIT ONE · ADMIT ONE

A Cotton-Top Tamarin Clinging To A Tree

©Jeremy Horner/CORBIS

Colombia has an amazing variety of plants and animals. In fact, for its size, Colombia has more plant and animal **species** than any other place in the world!

Along the coasts are mangrove trees and swaying coconut palms. The mountains have thick forests of mahogany, pine, rubber, and other trees. Hidden among the trees are orchids and other beautiful flowers. In the Amazon rain forest, thousands of other kinds of trees, grasses, and plants can be found.

Each different area has its own fascinating wildlife. On land there are jaguars, monkeys, deer, bears, snakes, and otters. Colombia has many different kinds of birds— in fact, over 1,500 different kinds! The oceans off the coast are teeming with fish, electric eels, and other sea creatures that live among the coral reefs and rocks.

Trees Growing In A Flat Area of Colombia

©Kevin Schafer/CORBIS

La Planada
Nature Reserve

A Spectacled
Bear At
La Planada
Nature
Reserve

A 19th Century Drawing Of Colombians In Quito

Cartagena

Quito

Huila

Long Ago

People have lived in Colombia for thousands of years. Early Native Americans farmed, hunted, lived in villages, and made beautiful artwork. In the early 1500s, European explorers landed in Colombia. Soon after that, people from Spain came to Colombia looking for gold.

The Spanish **enslaved** the Indians and took over their land. For the next 300 years, Spain ruled the area. In 1819, freedom fighter Simón Bolívar led Colombia to independence from Spanish rule.

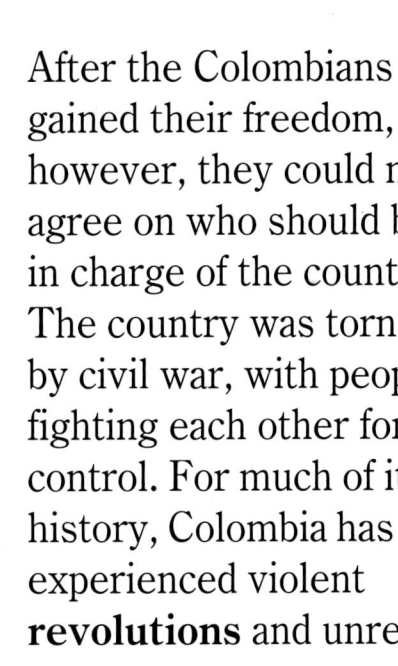

A Statue Of Christopher Columbus In Cartagena

©Jeremy Homer/CORBIS

A Tomb Sculpture In San Agustin Archaeological Park In Huila

After the Colombians gained their freedom, however, they could not agree on who should be in charge of the country. The country was torn by civil war, with people fighting each other for control. For much of its history, Colombia has experienced violent **revolutions** and unrest.

©Leonard de Selva/CORBIS

Colombia Today

Today, Columbia has a **democratic** government. The people elect a president and a **legislature** composed of a Senate and a House of Representatives. The legislators make and enforce the nation's laws.

©Jeremy Horner/CORBIS

Anti-Drug Police In Bogotá

Hall Of Congress In Bogotá

©Jeremy Horner/CORBIS

Colombia still faces serious problems, however. Many people are unhappy, and crime and fighting are still common. Colombia's biggest problem comes from drugs. Large, well-organized groups of Colombians produce and sell illegal drugs made from plants grown in the country. The government is trying hard to stop them, but Colombia's drug dealers still sell drugs all over the world.

©Jeremy Horner/CORBIS

★ Bogotá

A Farmer In
Ibague

★Bogotá
•Ibague
•Silvia

©Jeremy Horner/CORBIS

The People

Most Colombians today are *mestizos* (mess-TEE-zos) of mixed Native American and European backgrounds. Other Colombians are *mulattoes* (moo-LAH-tohz) with mixed African and European backgrounds. Native Indian groups make up only a very small part of the country's population.

The number of people in Colombia is growing every year, which means there are lots of young people. In fact, one out of every three Colombians is a child!

A Traditionally Dressed Guambiano Indian Woman In Silvia

©Jeremy Horner/CORBIS

Children Laughing In Bogotá

©The Purcell Team/CORBIS

For many Colombians, religion is a very important part of their lives. Nine out of every ten Colombians belong to the Roman Catholic faith. In fact, Catholicism is the nation's official religion. Its influence is felt in education, values, and everyday life.

City Life
And
Country
Life

Most of Colombia's people live in cities, which are much like cities elsewhere. Some wealthy city dwellers drive nice cars and live in fancy homes. Other people live in terrible **poverty**, without enough money for proper shelter and food. Some Colombians, many of them children, are so poor that they live on the city streets. They try to survive by doing odd jobs, begging, or even stealing.

Life in Colombia's countryside is much simpler than life in the city. Good jobs are scarce, however, so many people are poor. In fact, many country dwellers live without adequate sewers or even running water. To escape this poverty, many move to the city, looking for a better life.

Some Native American peoples still live in the more hidden parts of the Colombian countryside. They live much as their ancestors did hundreds of years ago.

Main Street In Cartagena

©Enzo & Paolo Ragazzini/CORBIS

Cartagena

★Bogotá

Bogotá At Night

©Omar Bechara Baruque; Eye Ubiquitous/CORBIS

Girls
Learning A
Foreign Language
In A Bogotá
High
School

Santa Marta
Cartagena
★Bogotá

©The Purcell Team/CORBIS

School in Colombian cities is a lot like school in the United States. In primary school, children learn how to read, write, and do math and science. Students must also learn about Catholicism. After elementary school, they can go to high school and even to college.

In the countryside, some children cannot go to school because they must work with their parents or because there are no schools nearby.

A University Student In Cartagena

©Owen Franken/CORBIS

A Street Vendor Sorting Oysters In Santa Marta

©The Purcell Team/CORBIS

The official language of Colombia is Spanish, which is also spoken in neighboring countries. Some people, however, still speak the Native American languages and **dialects** their families spoke hundreds of years ago. These native languages include Barasana, Cacua, Carapana, and Piapoco.

A Man Picking Coffee Beans In Chinchina

About one-quarter of Colombia's people work in farming, logging in the forests, or fishing along the coasts. Farmers grow a variety of crops, including sugarcane, potatoes, tobacco, and bananas. Colombia's most famous food crop is coffee. The mild coffee beans grown on Colombia's mountain slopes are some of the most popular in the world.

Another one-quarter of Colombia's people work in industry. Colombian factories make everything from cotton goods to tires to medicine. Some Colombians work deep in mines looking for gold, silver, or rare emeralds. Most of the remaining workers have jobs in banks, offices, restaurants, shops, and other businesses.

© The Purcell Team/CORBIS

A Man Operating Machines In A Printing Plant In Cali

© The Purcell Team/CORBIS

Manaure

Chinchina

Cali

Salt Miners In Manaure

A Vendor Selling Bananas At A Market In Tunja

• Tunja
• Cachipay
• Cali

Food

Colombia's foods are as varied as the land itself. Most meals are made with some combination of chicken, pork, fish, potatoes, rice, and beans. A common meal is *ajiaco de pollo (ah-HYAH-koh day POH-yoh),* a potato, vegetable, and chicken stew. Besides the main dish, Colombians eat a lot of soups and fresh fruit. Of course, at every meal there is plenty of Colombian-grown coffee!

©Jeremy Horner/CORBIS

Fruits And Vegetables At A Produce Stand Near Cachipay

A Woman Cooking Traditional Food In Cali

©The Purcell Team/CORBIS

Besides these traditional meals, each region has its own special foods. In some places you can find pigeon soup, cooked guinea pig, or even big fried ants! Large cities have restaurants that serve Chinese, Italian, or other foods—and even hamburgers and fries.

Musicians Playing At The Festival Of The Devil In Riosucio

©Jeremy Horner/CORBIS

Colombians like to spend time outside enjoying their beautiful land. People have fun swimming, golfing, or playing games such as baseball or basketball. The most popular sport, however, is soccer. Soccer matches draw huge crowds of excited fans.

Day-to-day life is hard, and people like to have fun on holidays and festivals. Most Colombian holidays celebrate religious events. The biggest holiday is a festival called Carnival. Carnival starts before the religious season of Lent and lasts for many days. During Carnival, the entire country enjoys food, parades, games and dances.

Boys Watching A Soccer Match On TV In Barranquila

©Jeremy Horner/CORBIS

With so many wonderful sights and sounds, Colombia is a fascinating country. Maybe someday you can visit Colombia and see its beautiful mountains and lively cities.

A Bullfight In Bogotá

GARGANTA LA VOZ !

Car

OMEGA

Nº14-79 TEL 472-412

BARE

Area
Almost 441,000 square miles
(1,142,000 square kilometers)—about the size of Washington, Oregon,
California, and Nevada combined.

Population
About 40 million people.

Capital City
Bogotá.

Other Important Cities
Cali, Medellín, Barranquila, and Cartagena.

Money
The Colombian peso.

National Language
Spanish.

National Song
"Himno Nacional," or "National Anthem."

National Holiday
Independence Day on July 20th.

National Flag
The flag has three stripes. The yellow stripe stands for Colombia's land, the
blue stripe stands for the rivers and nearby oceans, and the red stripe stands
for the people killed fighting for Colombia's independence.

Head of State and Head of Government
The president of Colombia.

Official Name
República de Colombia (The Republic of Colombia).

Colombia Trivia

Did You Know?

Choco, an area in western Colombia, gets rain almost every day. In fact, it averages 27 feet of rain every year! That makes Choco one of the wettest places on Earth.

Colombia is the only nation in North, Central, or South America named after explorer Christopher Columbus.

Near the city of Zipaquira, a huge mountain has been mined for rock salt. Inside the mountain, the miners carved a church as they took out the salt. The main room has a 75-foot ceiling and room for 10,000 people! The statues in the church are all carved out of salt.

A full-grown coffee tree can produce about 2,000 coffee berries each year—enough for only 1 pound of coffee. The farmers who grow the coffee must pick each berry by hand.

How Do You Say?

	SPANISH	HOW TO SAY IT
Hello	hola	OH–lah
Good-bye	adiós	ah–dee–OHS
Please	por favor	POR fah–VOR
Thank You	gracias	GRAH–see–uhs
One	uno	OO–noh
Two	dos	DOHS
Three	tres	TRACE
Colombia	Colombia	koh–LOHM–bee–ah

continents (KON-tih-nents)
Earth's continents are large land areas surrounded mostly by oceans. The nation of Colombia is on the continent of South America.

democratic (deh-muh-KRA-tik)
When the government of a country is democratic, the people elect their leaders. Colombia has a democratic government.

dialects (DY-uh-lekts)
A dialect is a different form of a language spoken by people in a certain area. Some people in Colombia speak Native American dialects.

enslaved (en-SLAYVD)
To enslave people is to force them to work for you and never pay them or let them leave. Spanish settlers enslaved Colombia's native peoples.

equator (ee-KWAY-ter)
The equator is an imaginary line that runs around the center of Earth and divides it in half. The equator crosses southern Colombia.

legislature (LEJ-iss-lay-tchur)
A legislature is a group of elected leaders who make a nation's laws. Colombia has a legislature.

poverty (POV-er-tee)
People who live in poverty have too little money for food, shelter, clothing, and other basic needs. Some people in Colombia live in extreme poverty.

revolutions (rev-oh-LOO-shunz)
Revolutions are sudden, often violent uprisings to change a government. Colombia has experienced a number of revolutions.

species (SPEE-sheez)
A species is a separate kind of a plant or animal. Colombia has an enormous number of plant and animal species.

tropical (TROP-ih-kull)
Tropical lands have warm, moist weather all year. Parts of Colombia have a tropical climate.

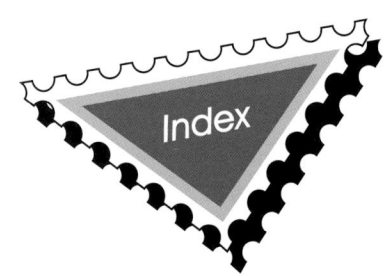

Index

Amazon rain forest, 9, 10

Andes Mountains, 9

animals, 10

Bolívar, Simón, 13

cities, 18, 21, 25, 26, 28

coffee, 22, 25, 30

continents, 6

crops, 22

dialects, 21

drug trade, 14

education, 17, 21

equator, 9

factories, 22

farming, 22

foods, 22, 25

government, 14, 28

history, 13, 14

holidays, 26, 28

land, 6, 9, 10, 13, 26, 28

languages, 21

llanos, 9

mestizos, 17

mulattoes, 17

Native Americans, 13, 17, 18, 21

pastimes, 26

people, 9, 13, 14, 17, 18, 21, 22, 26, 28, 30

plants, 10, 14

poverty, 18

religion, 17

revolutions, 14

Spain, 13

sports, 26

weather, 9

work, 21, 22

Web Sites

Learn more about Colombia!

Visit our homepage for lots of links about Colombia:

http://www.childsworld.com/links.html

Note to Parents, Teachers, and Librarians:
We routinely verify our Web links to make sure they're safe, active sites—so encourage your readers to check them out!